FOR ORGANS, PIANOS & ELECTRONIC KEYBOARDS

E-Z PLAY TODAY

68

PIRATES of the CARIBBEAN

Disney characters and artwork © Disney Enterprises, Inc.

ISBN 978-1-4234-8289-5

**Walt Disney Music Company**
**Wonderland Music Company, Inc.**

DISTRIBUTED BY

HAL•LEONARD®
CORPORATION

7777 W. BLUEMOUND RD. P.O. BOX 13819 MILWAUKEE, WI 53213

In Australia contact:
**Hal Leonard Australia Pty. Ltd.**
4 Lentara Court
Cheltenham, Victoria, 3192 Australia
Email: ausadmin@halleonard.com.au

Visit Hal Leonard Online at
**www.halleonard.com**

# Blood Ritual/Moonlight Serenade

### from Walt Disney Pictures' PIRATES OF THE CARIBBEAN:
### THE CURSE OF THE BLACK PEARL

Registration 2
Rhythm: None

Music by Klaus Badelt

"Blood Ritual"

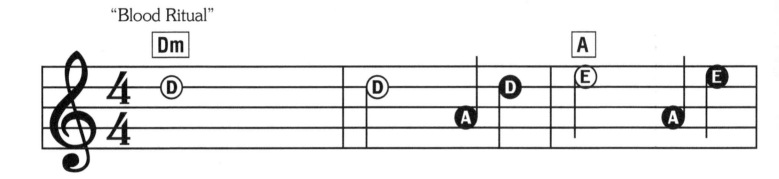

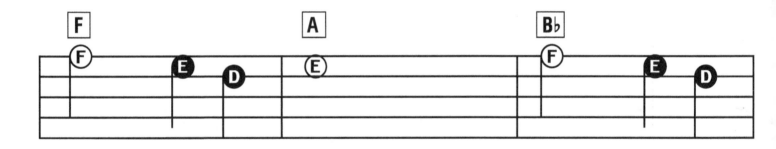

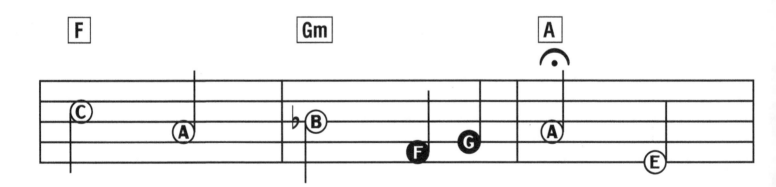

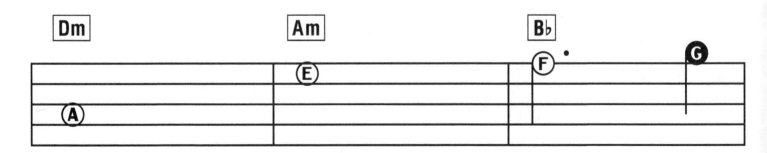

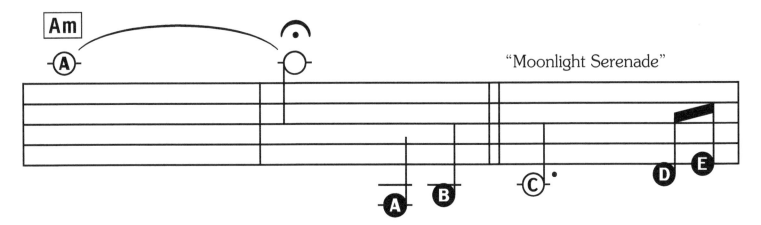

"Moonlight Serenade"

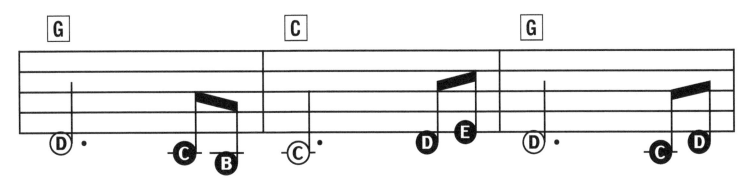

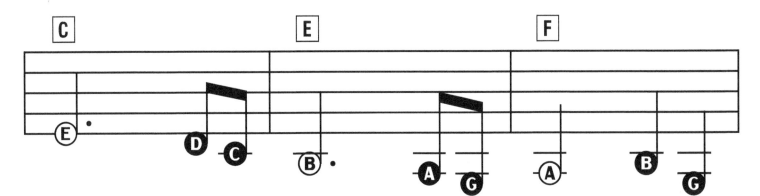

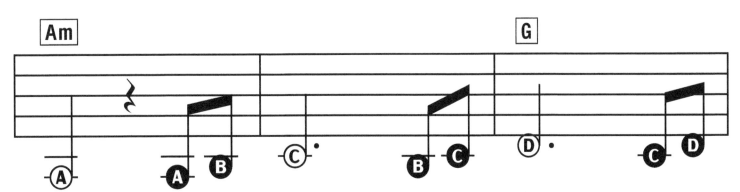

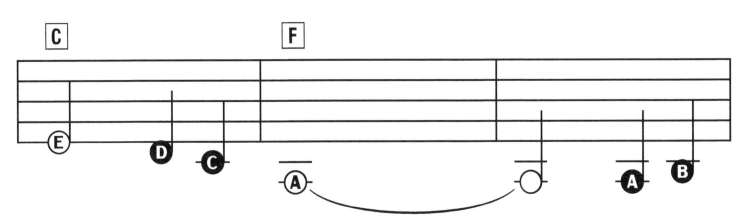

4

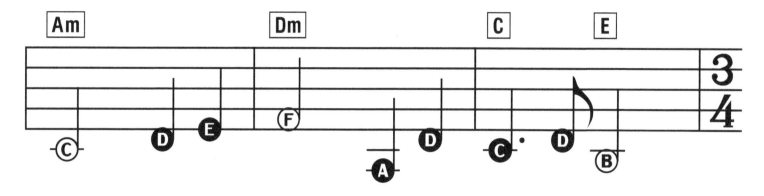

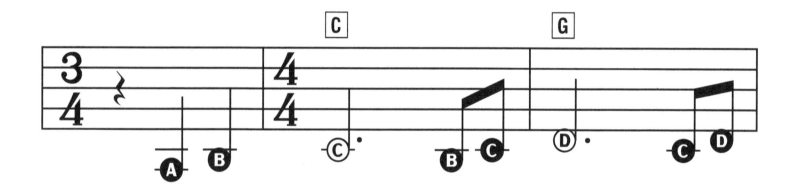

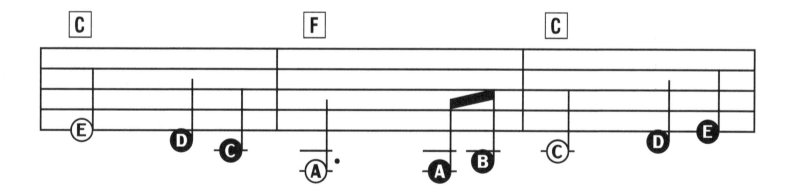

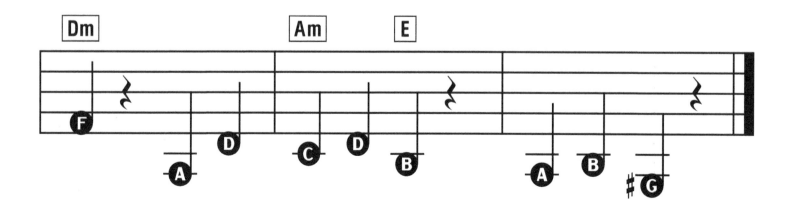

# The Medallion Calls
### from Walt Disney Pictures' PIRATES OF THE CARIBBEAN:
### THE CURSE OF THE BLACK PEARL

Registration 2
Rhythm: Waltz

Music by Klaus Badelt

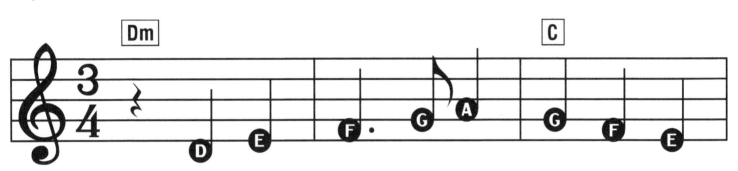

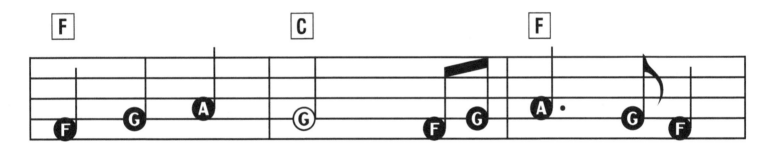

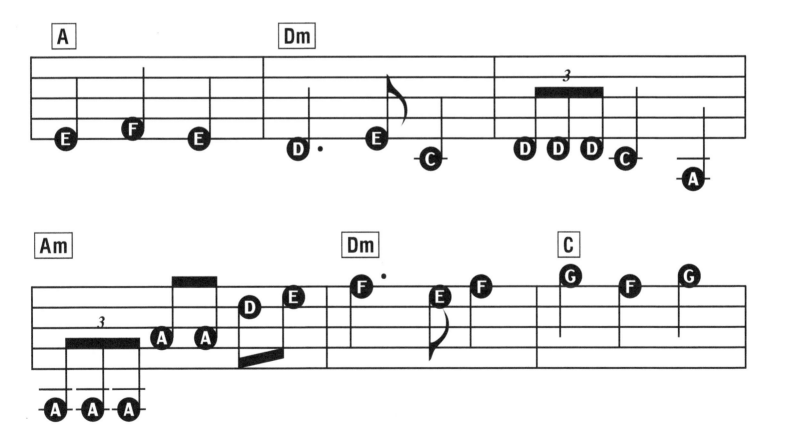

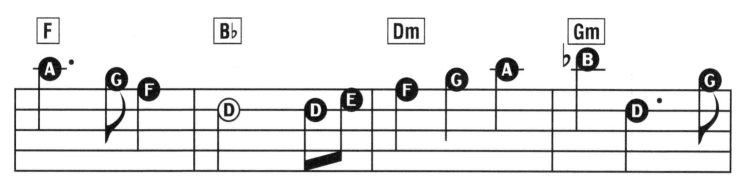

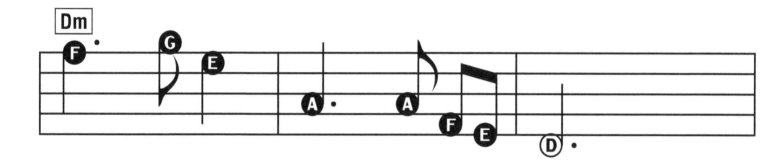

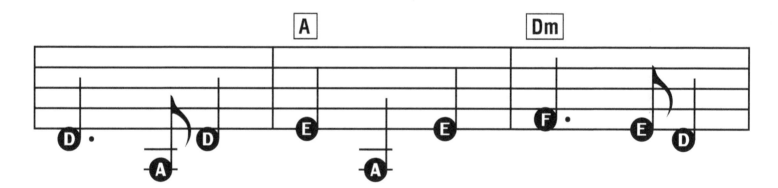

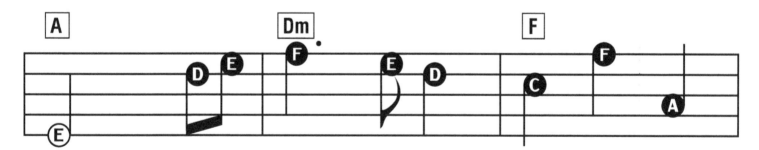

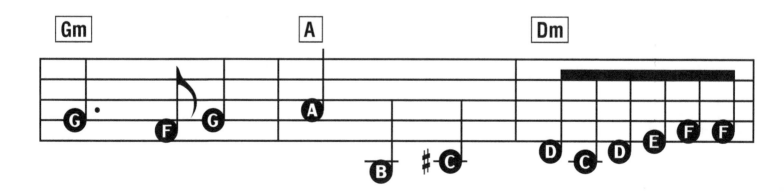

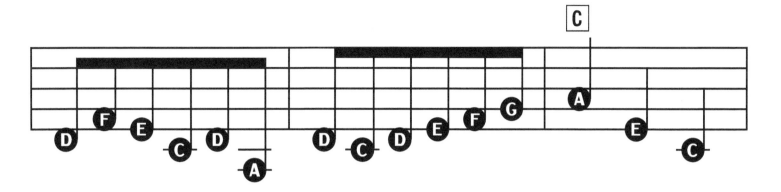

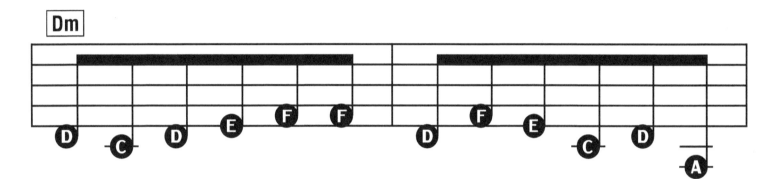

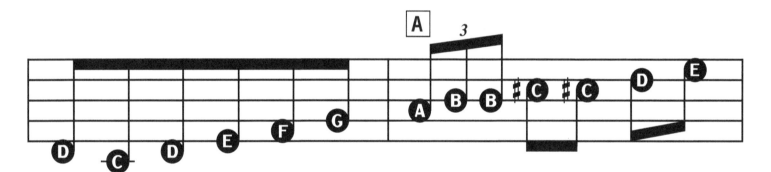

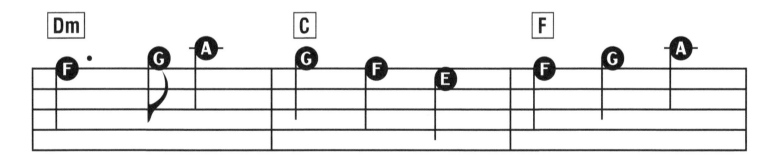

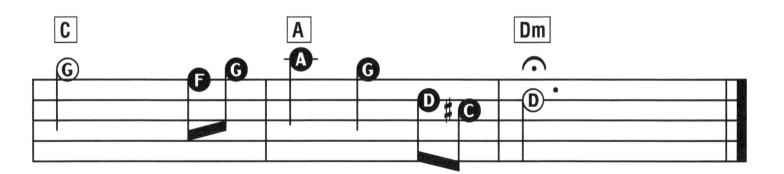

# Davy Jones

## from Walt Disney Pictures' PIRATES OF THE CARIBBEAN: DEAD MAN'S CHEST

Registration 3
Rhythm: Waltz

Music by Hans Zimmer

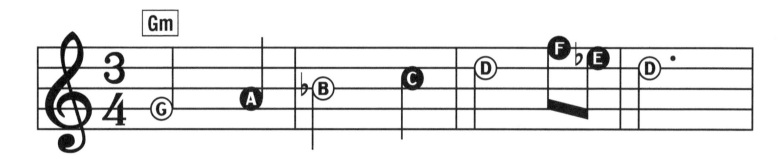

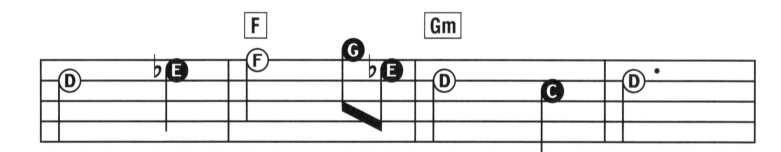

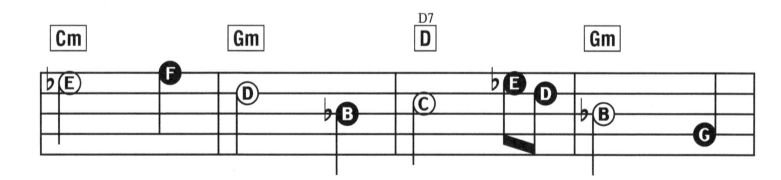

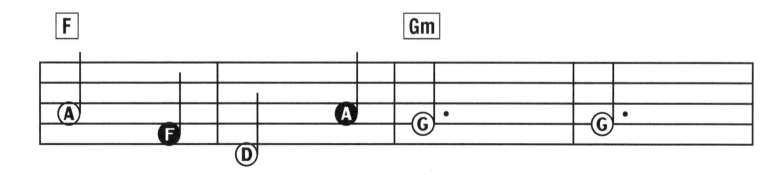

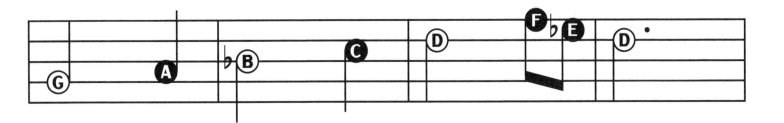

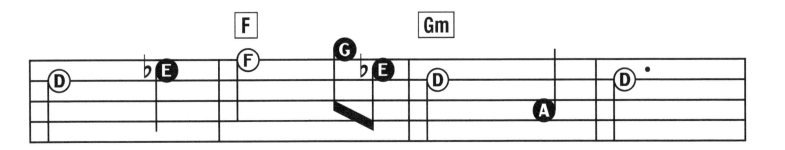

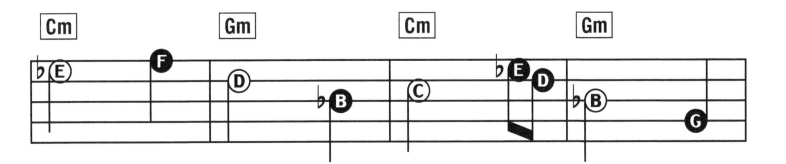

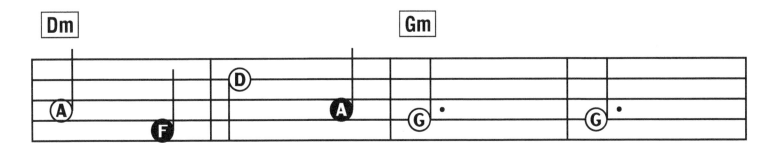

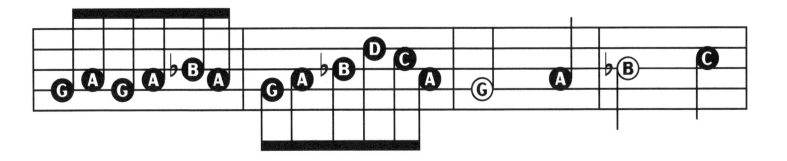

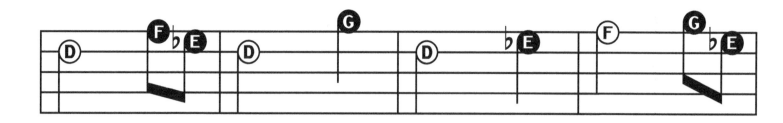

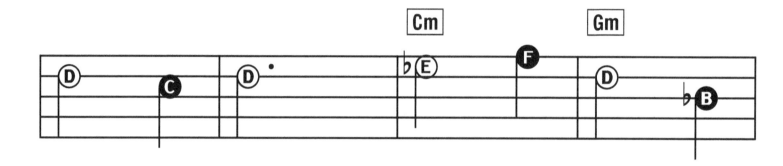

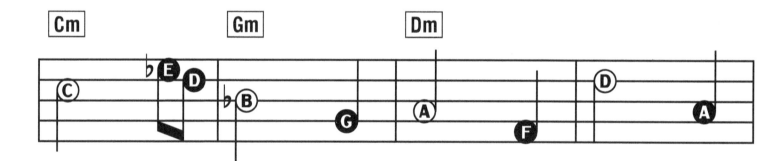

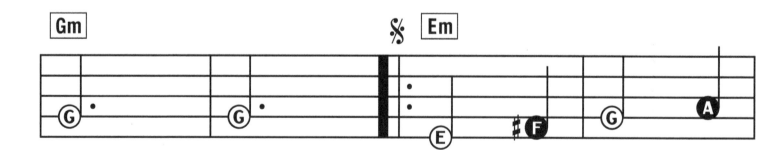

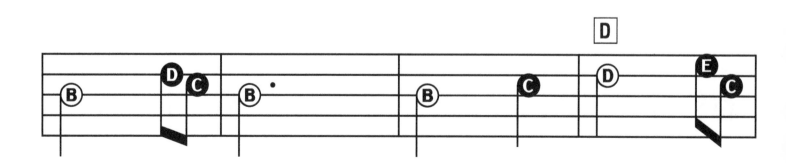

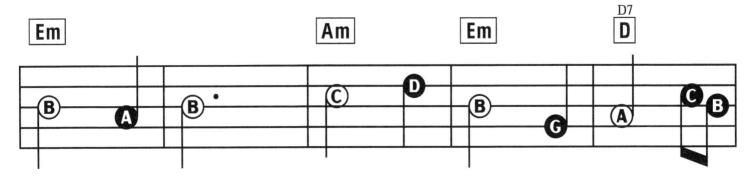

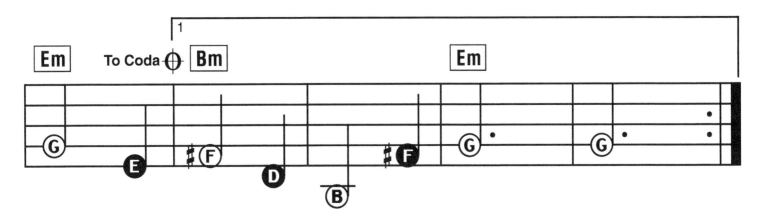

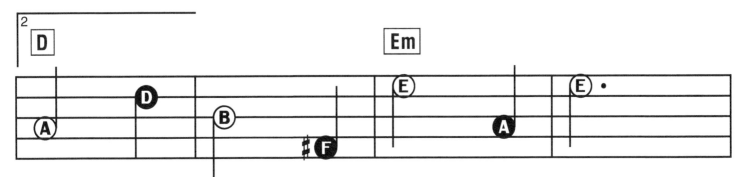

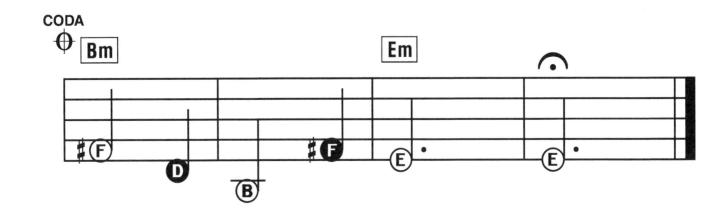

# He's a Pirate
## from Walt Disney Pictures' PIRATES OF THE CARIBBEAN:
## THE CURSE OF THE BLACK PEARL

Registration 7
Rhythm: Classical 6/8 or None

Music by Klaus Badelt

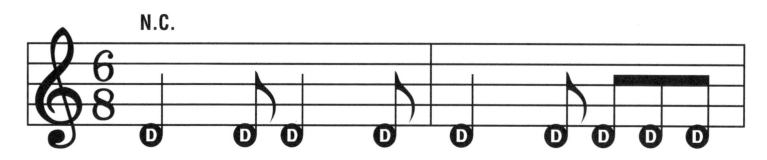

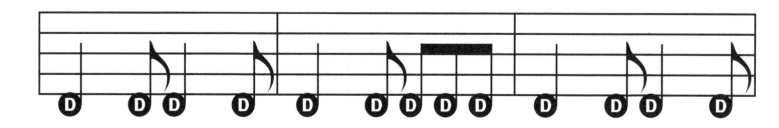

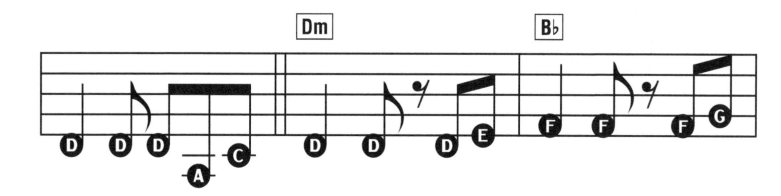

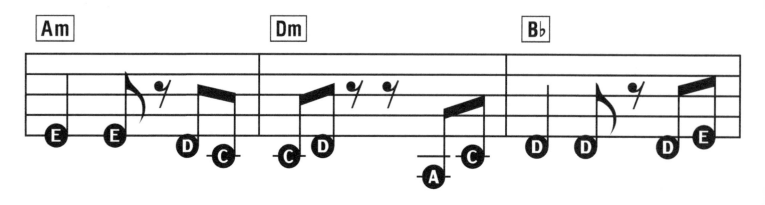

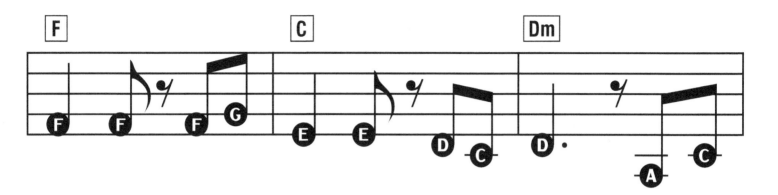

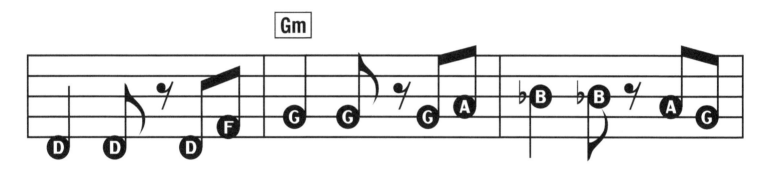

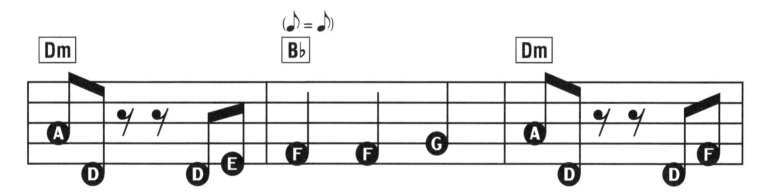

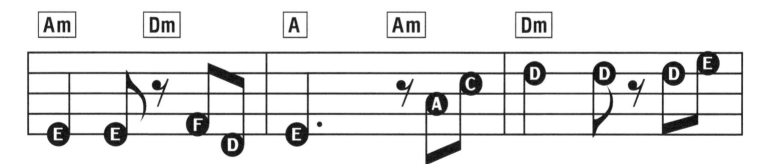

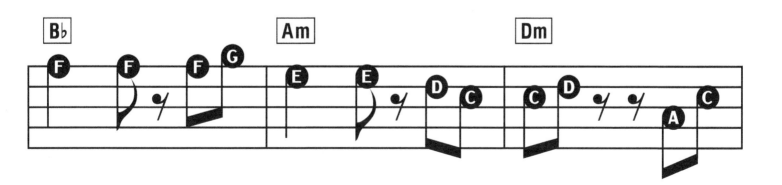

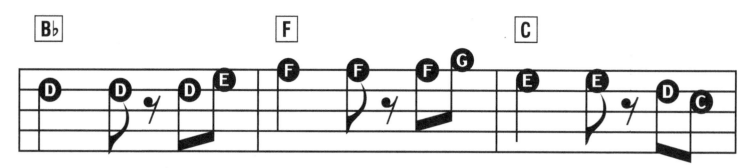

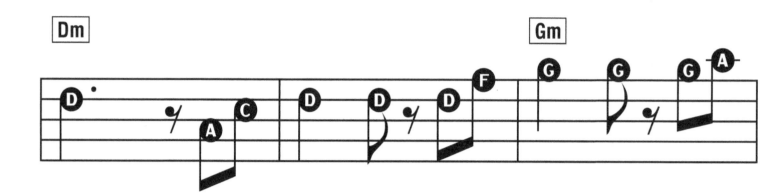

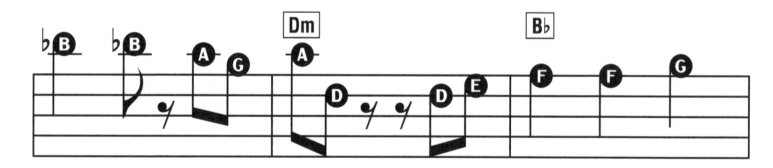

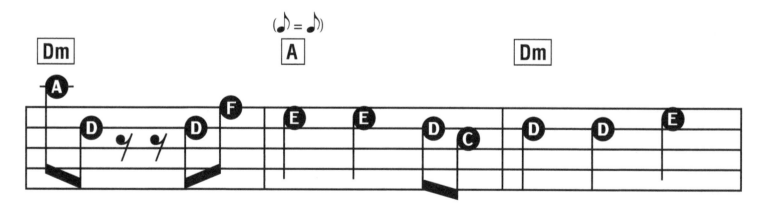

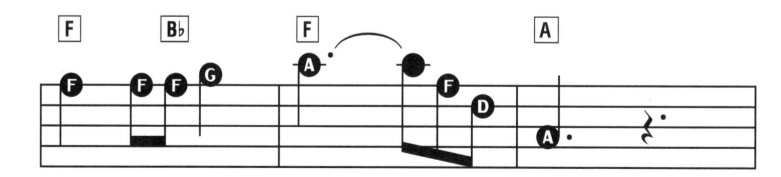

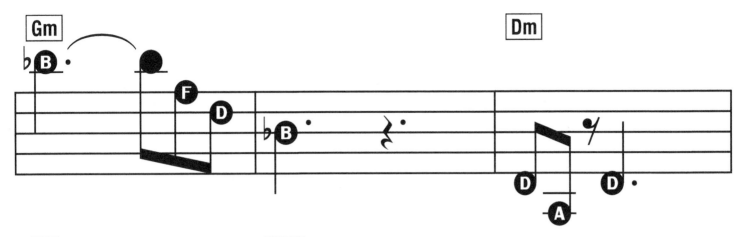

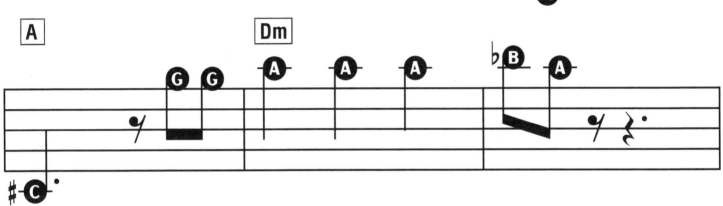

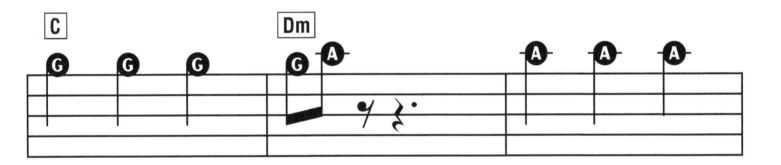

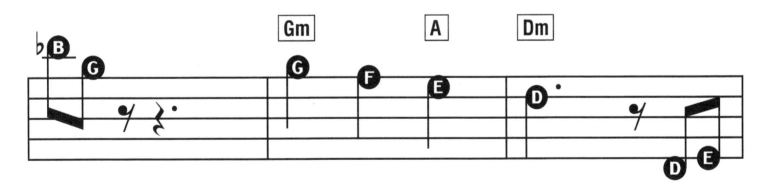

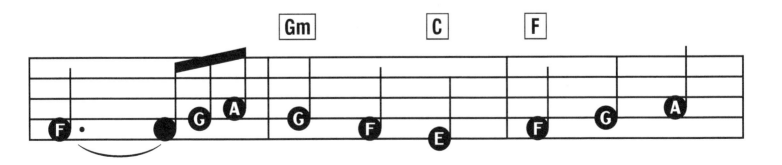

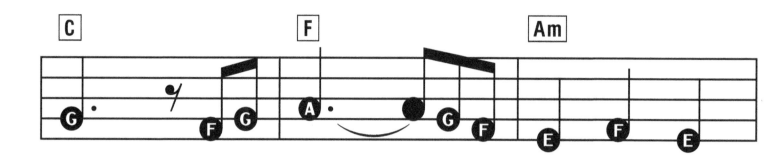

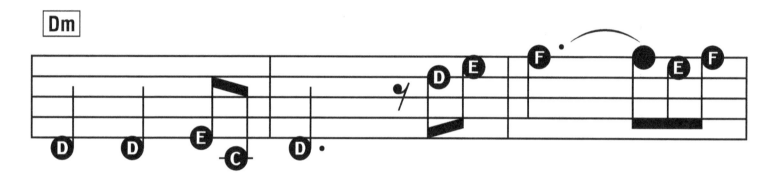

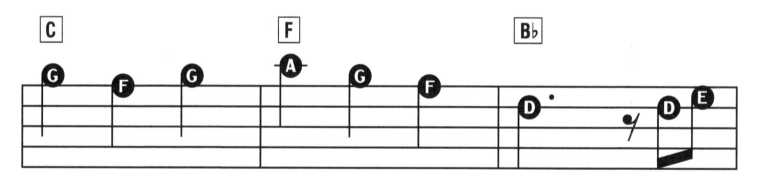

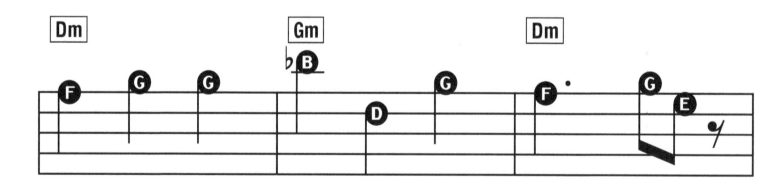

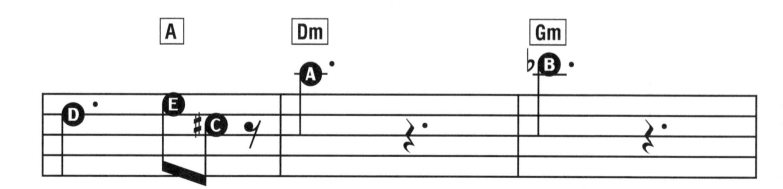

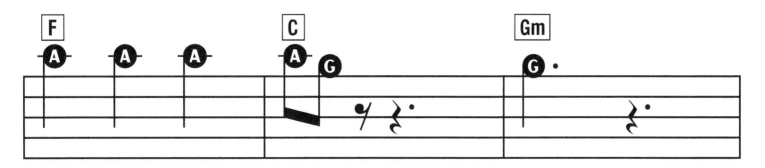

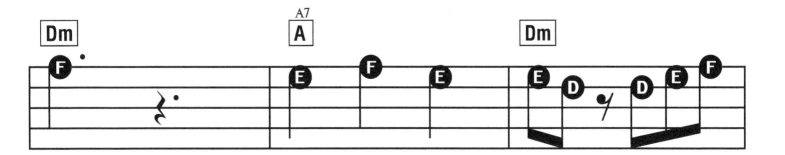

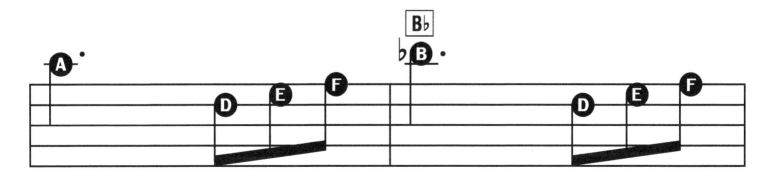

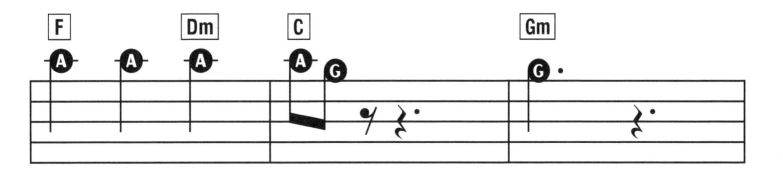

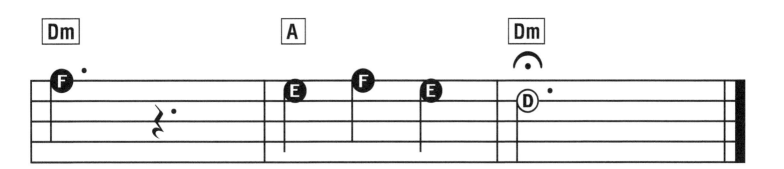

# Hoist the Colours

## from Walt Disney Pictures' PIRATES OF THE CARIBBEAN: AT WORLD'S END

Registration 2
Rhythm: None

Lyrics by Ted Elliot and Terry Rossio
Music by Hans Zimmer and Gore Verbinski

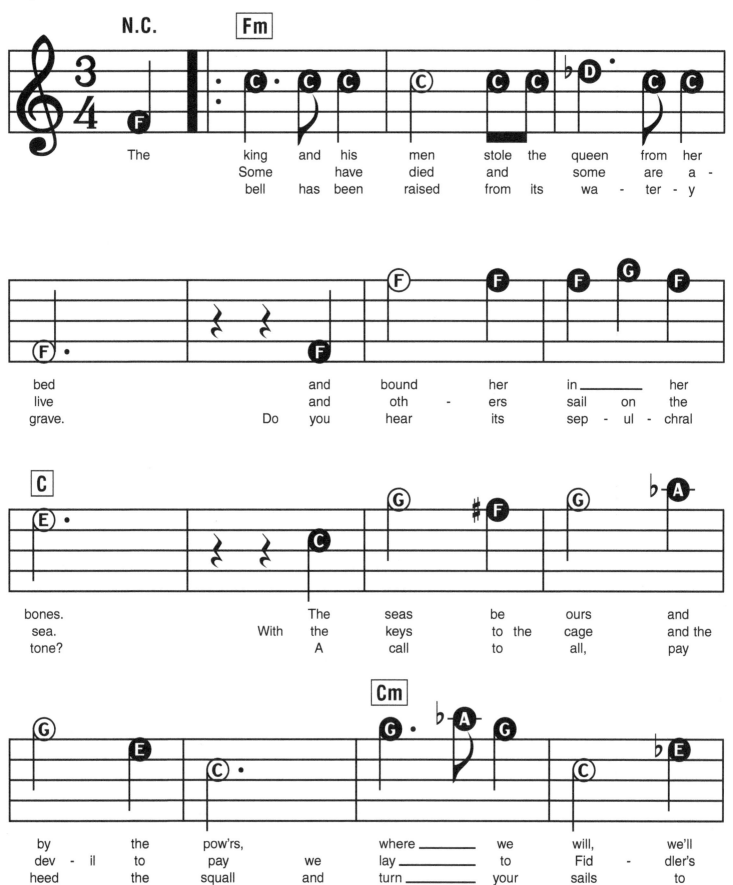

The king and his men stole the queen from her
Some have died and bound her in _____ her
bell has been raised and from its sail on the

bed and bound her in _____ her
live and oth - ers sail on the
grave. Do you hear its sep - ul - chral

bones. The seas be ours and
sea. With the keys to the cage and and the
tone? A call to all, pay

by the pow'rs, where _____ we will, we'll
dev - il to pay we lay _____ to Fid - dler's
heed the squall and turn _____ your sails to

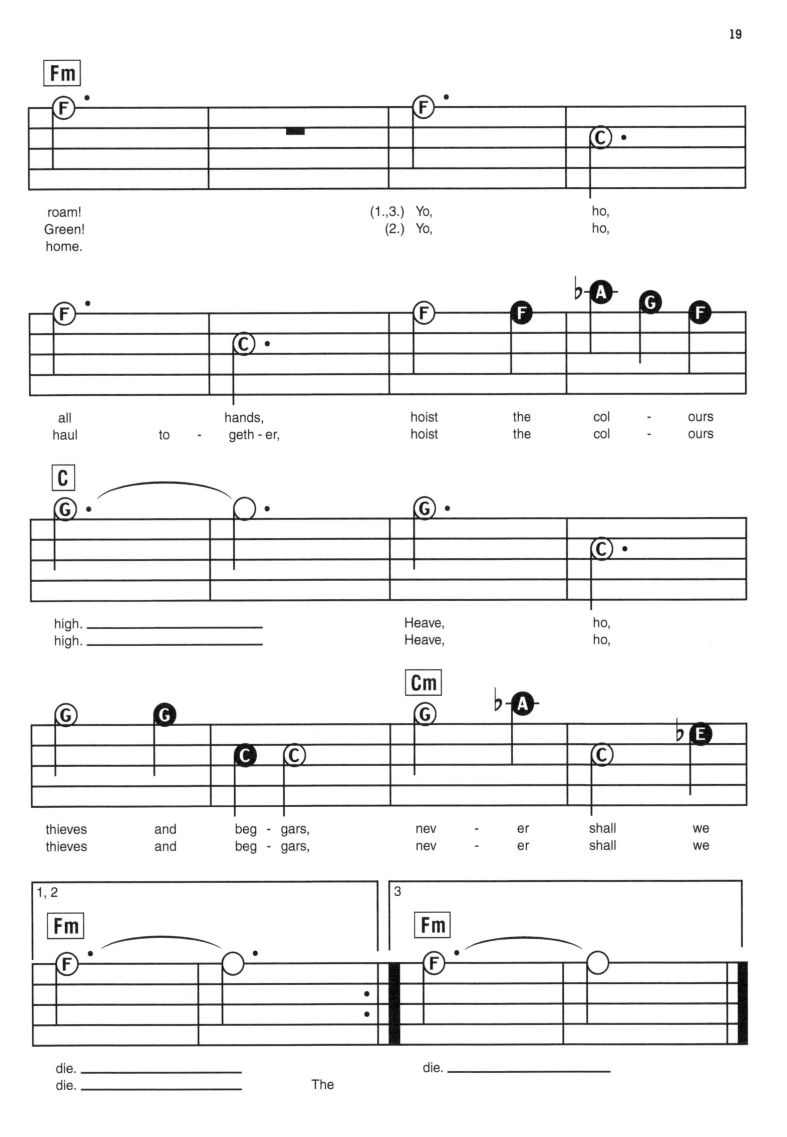

# I've Got My Eye on You

## from Walt Disney Pictures' PIRATES OF THE CARIBBEAN: DEAD MAN'S CHEST

Registration 8
Rhythm: Waltz

Music by Hans Zimmer

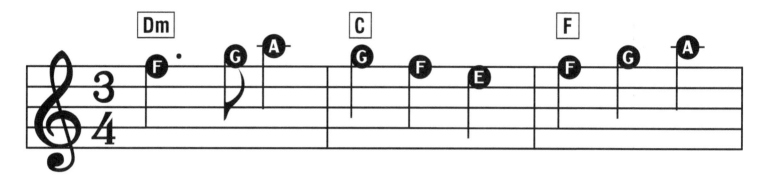

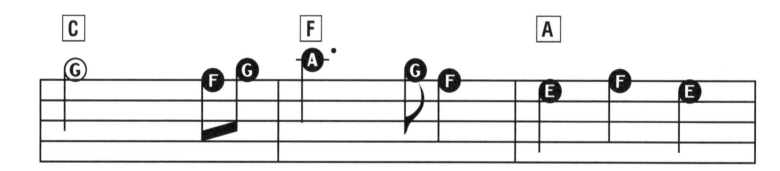

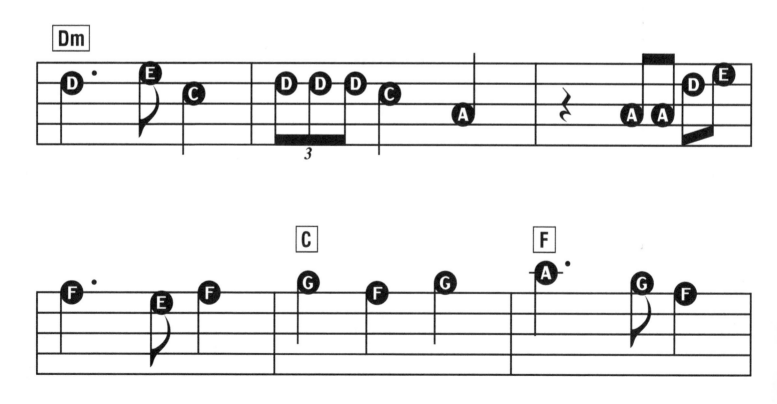

21

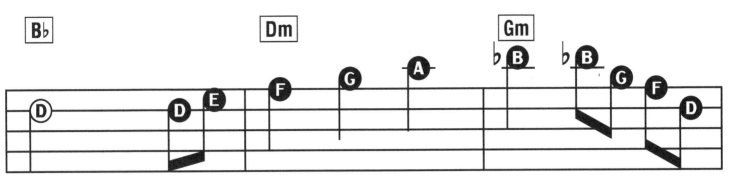

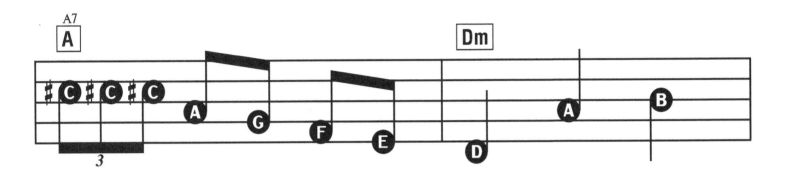

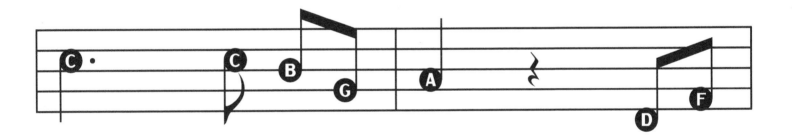

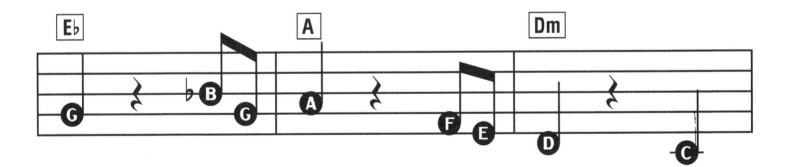

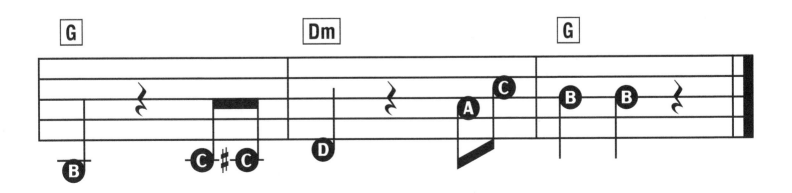

# One Day
## from Walt Disney Pictures' PIRATES OF THE CARIBBEAN: AT WORLD'S END

Registration 2
Rhythm: None

Music by Hans Zimmer

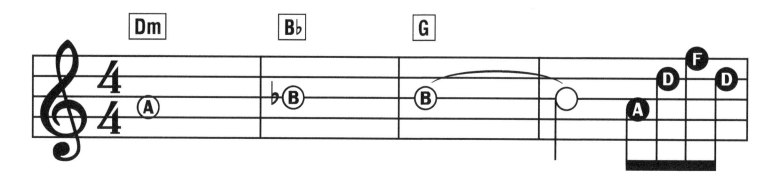

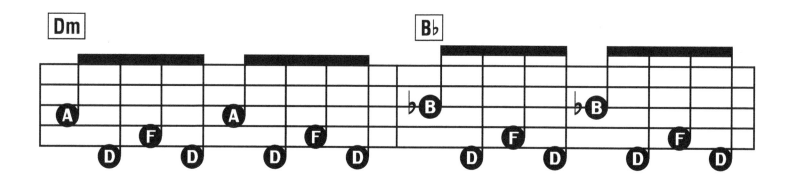

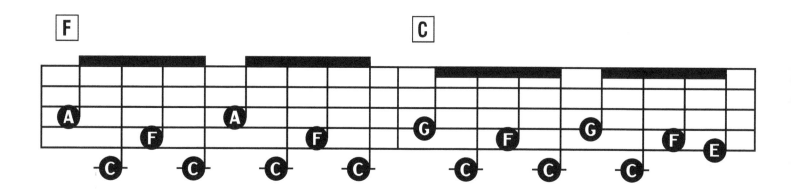

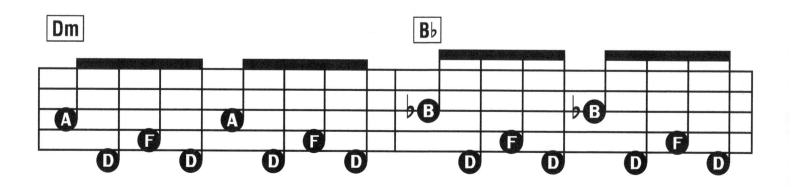

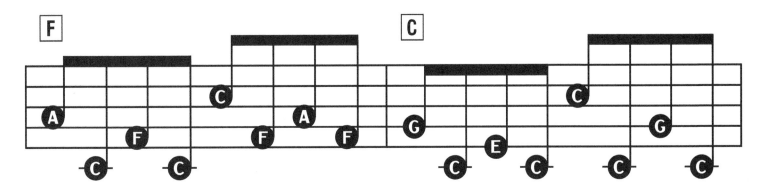

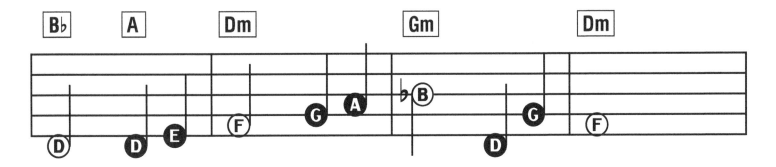

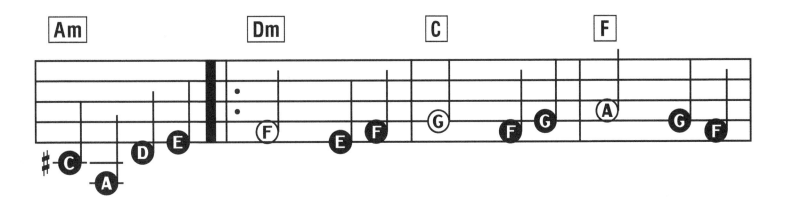

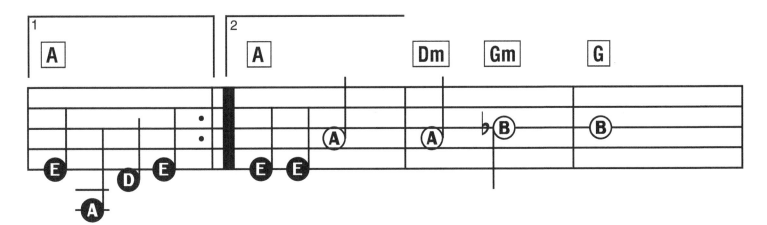

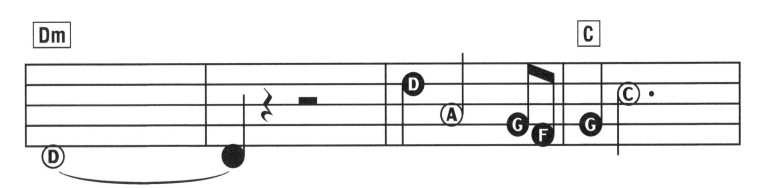

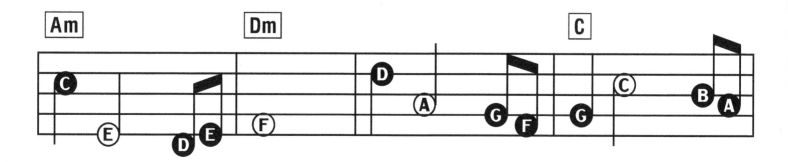

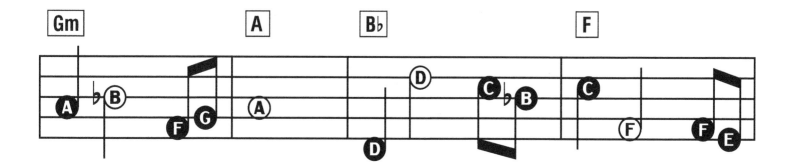

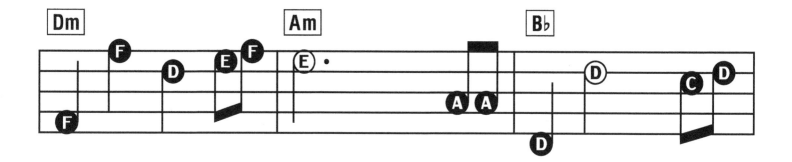

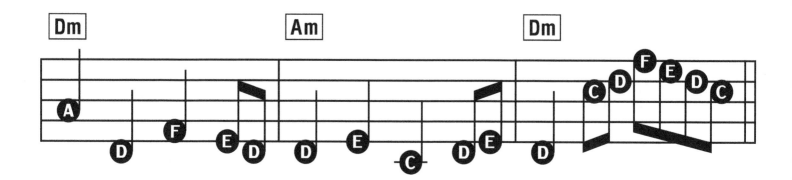

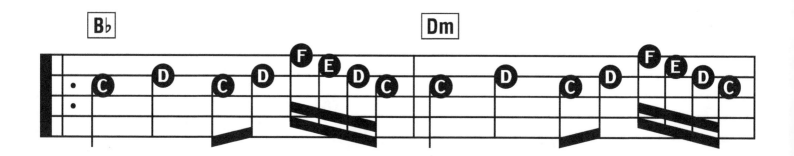

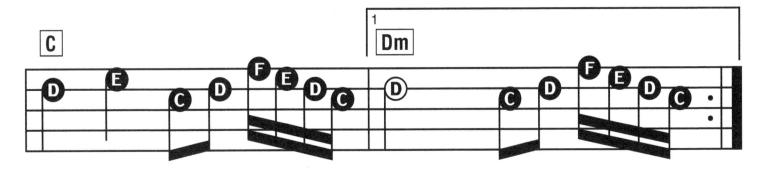

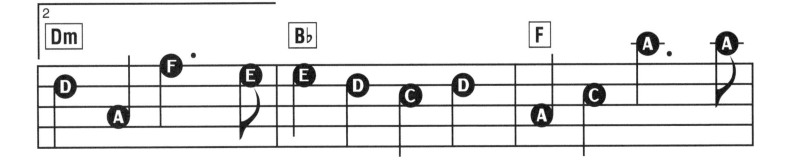

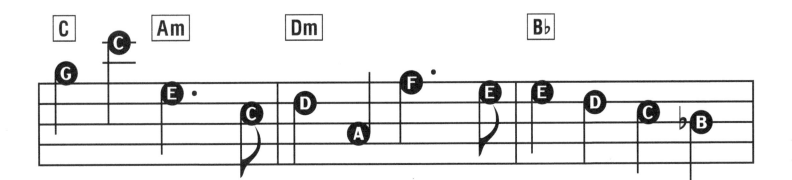

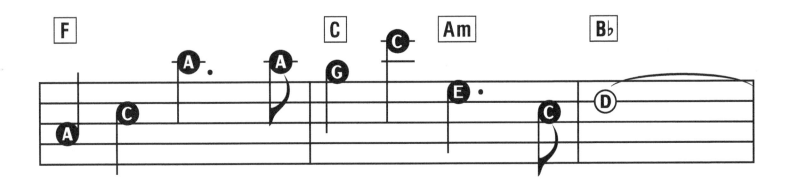

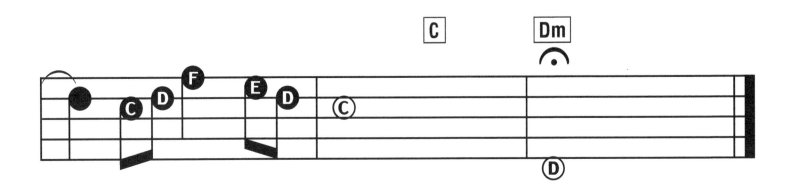

# Up Is Down
## from Walt Disney Pictures' PIRATES OF THE CARIBBEAN: AT WORLD'S END

Registration 1
Rhythm: Classical 6/8 or None

Music by Hans Zimmer

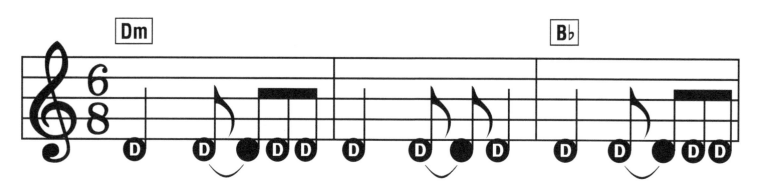

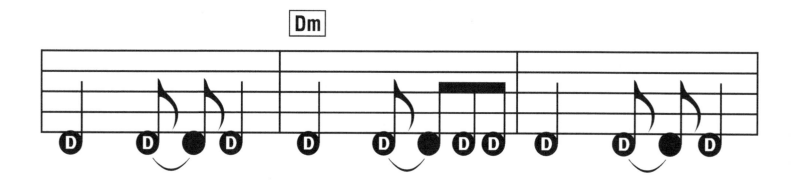

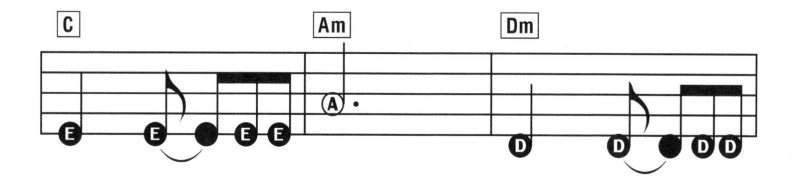

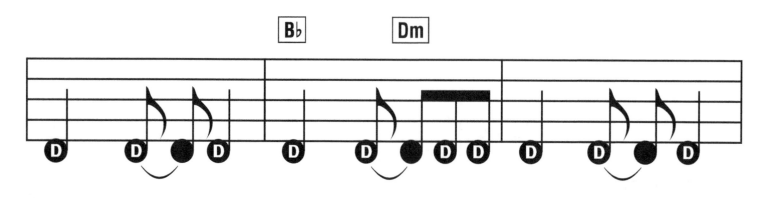

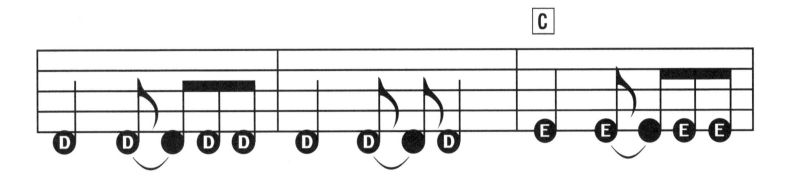

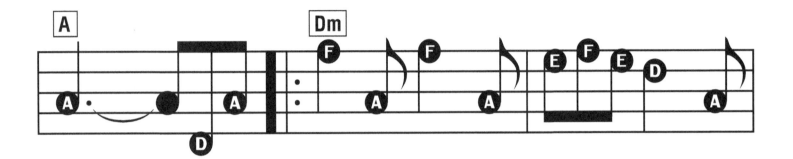

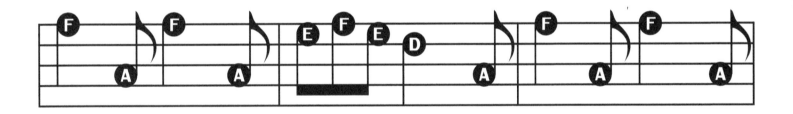

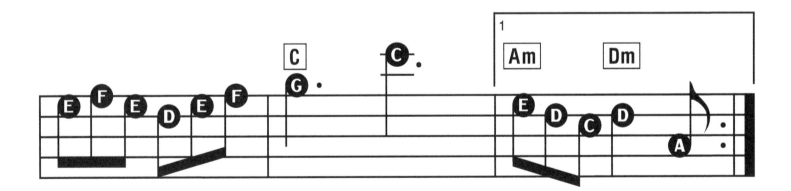

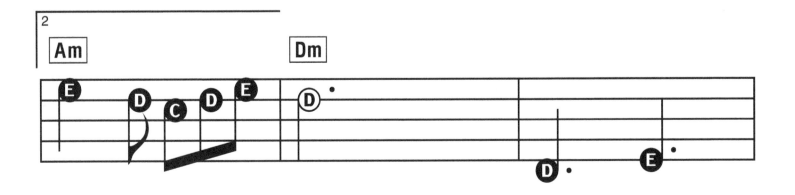

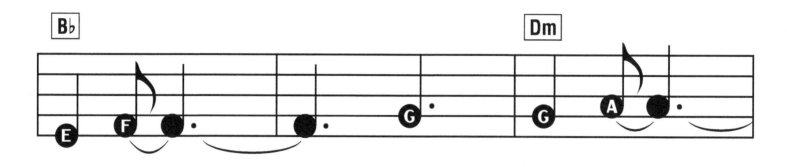

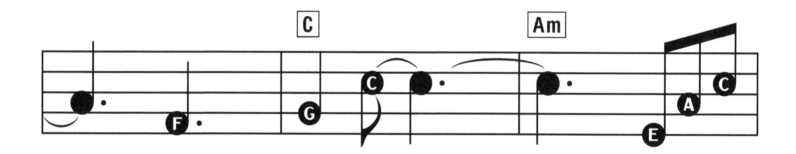

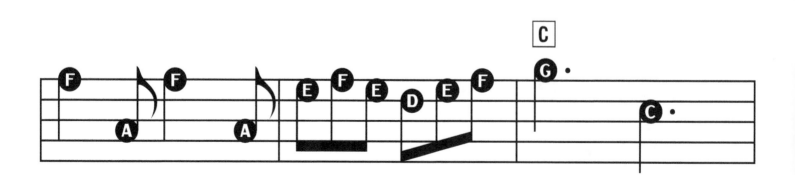

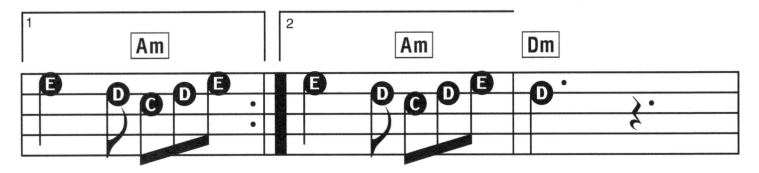

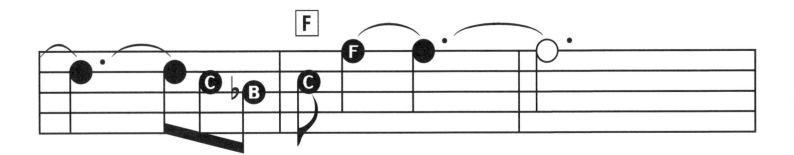
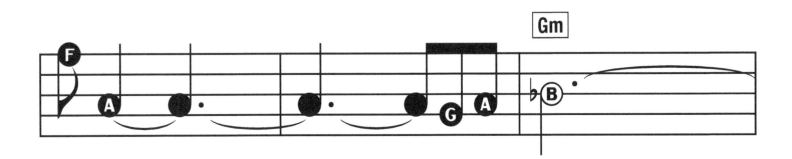
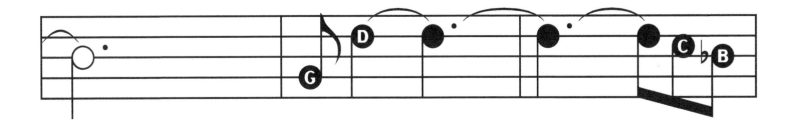

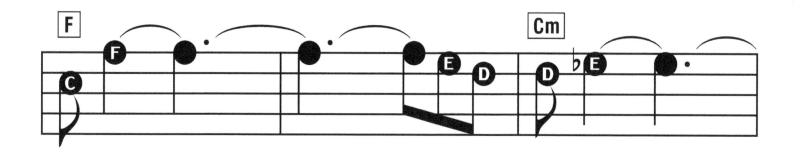

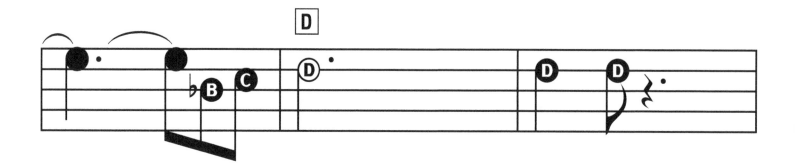

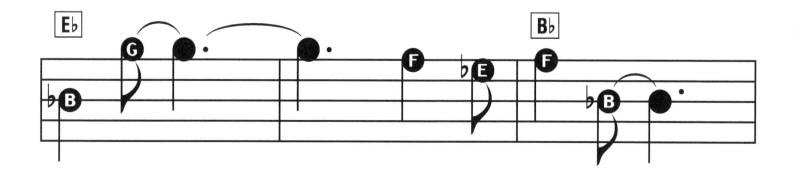

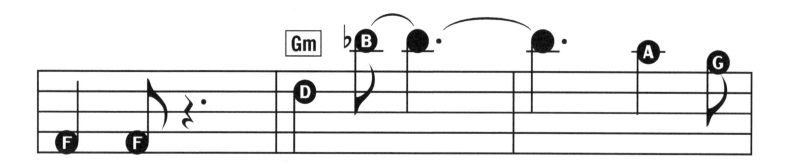

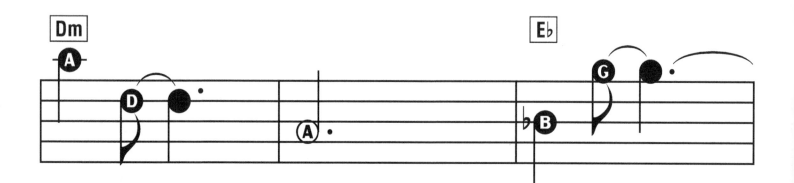

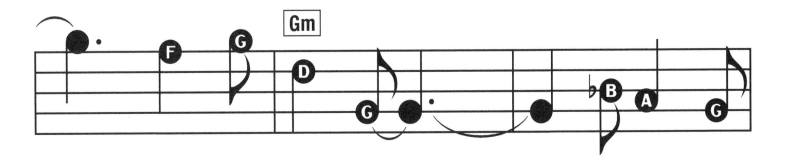

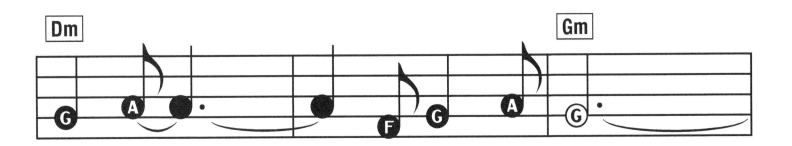

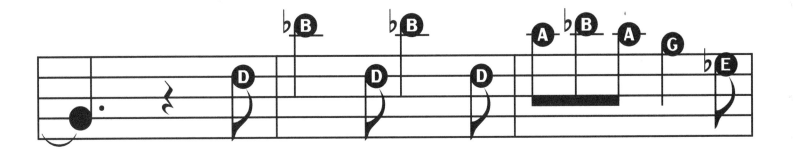

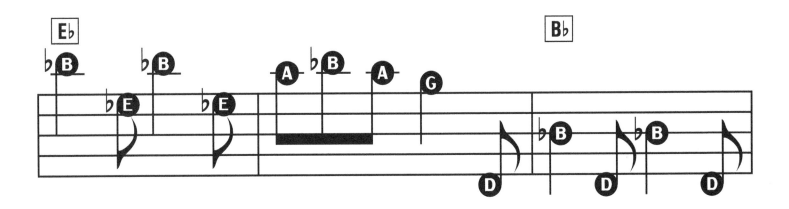

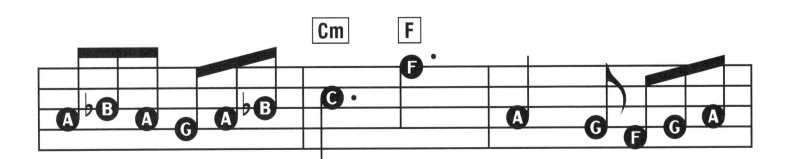

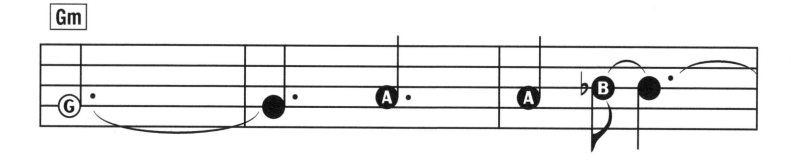

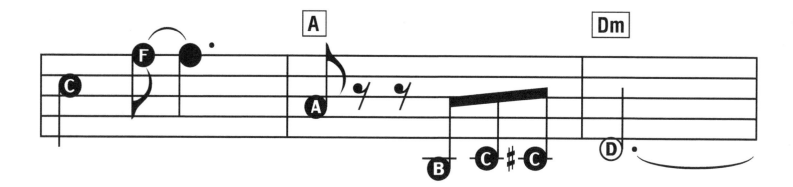

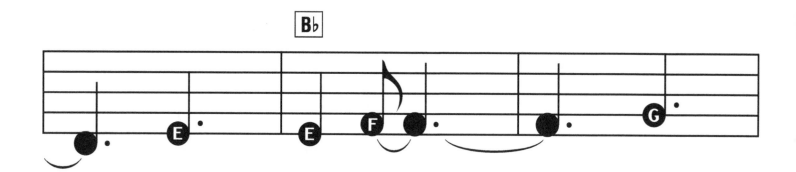

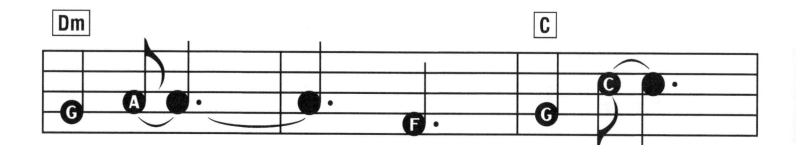

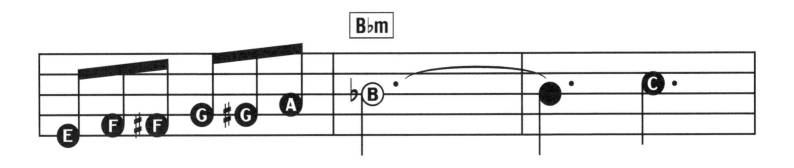

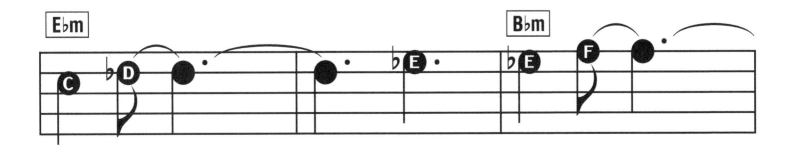

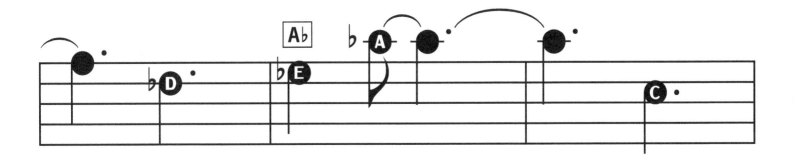

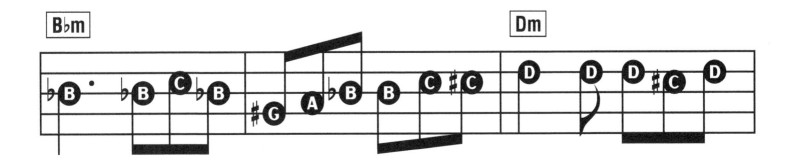

34

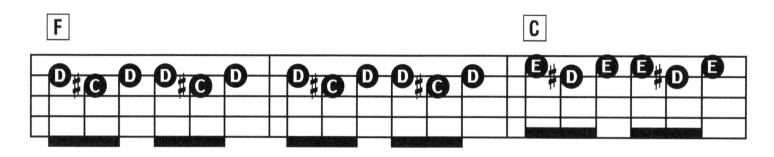

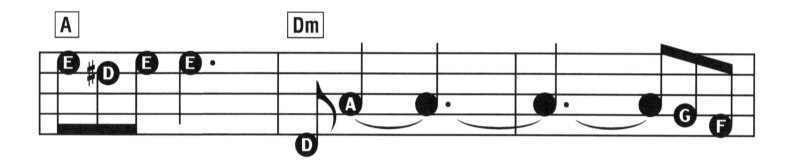

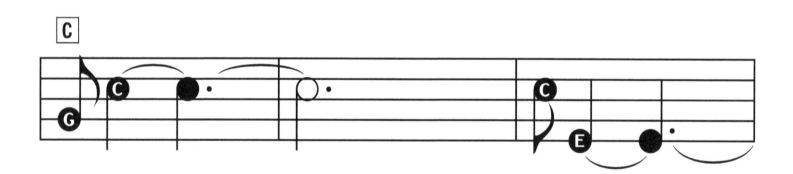

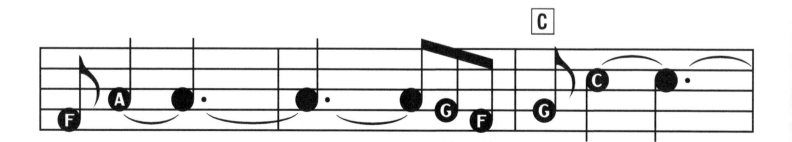

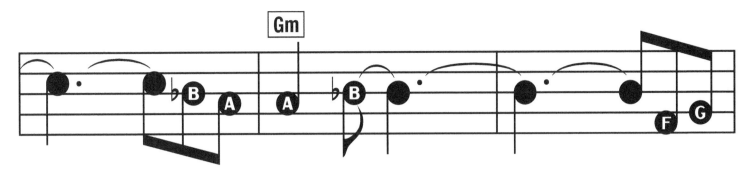

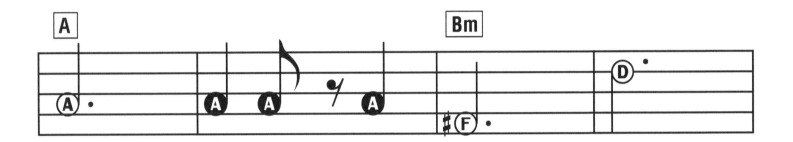

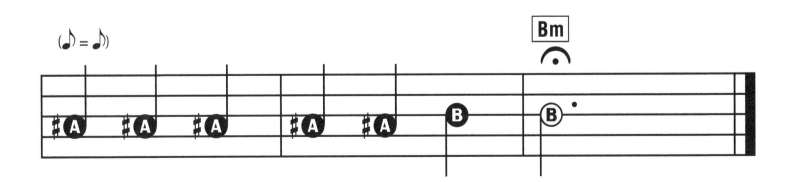

# Two Hornpipes
## (Fisher's Hornpipe)
### from Walt Disney Pictures' PIRATES OF THE CARIBBEAN: DEAD MAN'S CHEST

Registration 10
Rhythm: March

By Skip Henderson

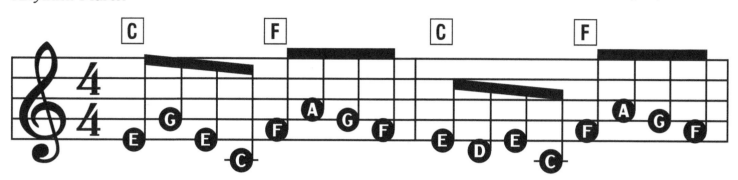

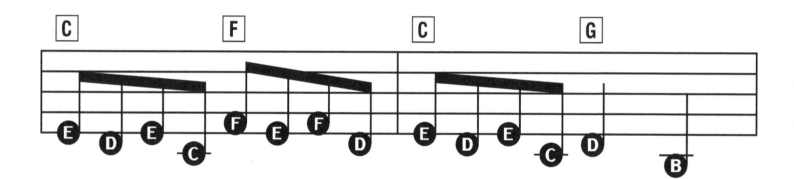

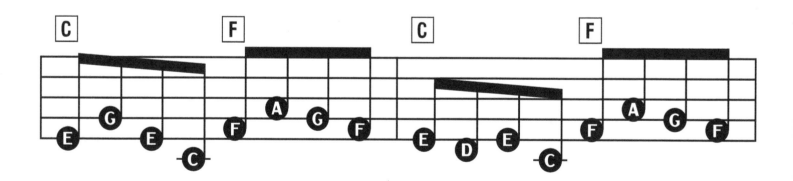

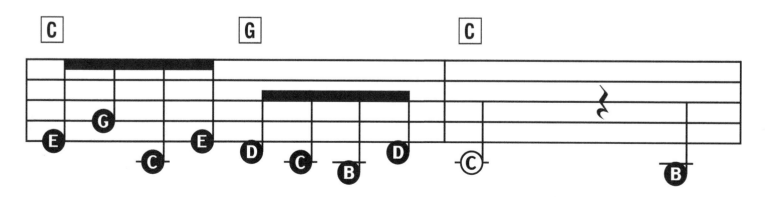

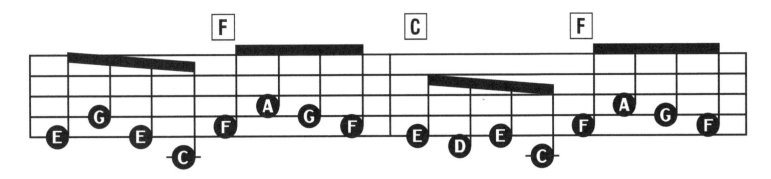

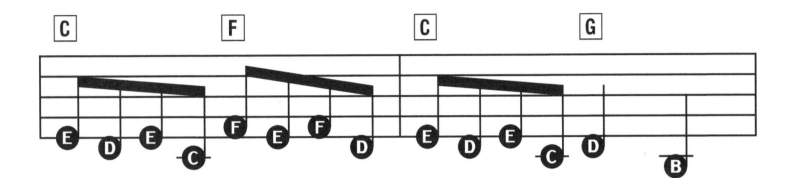

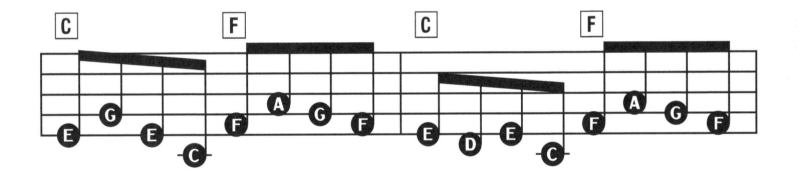

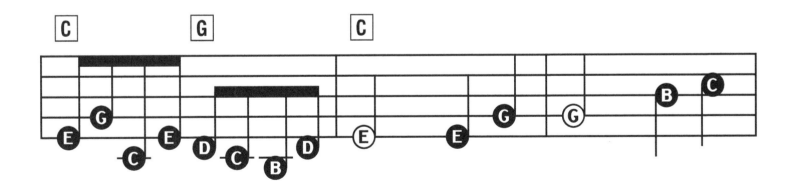

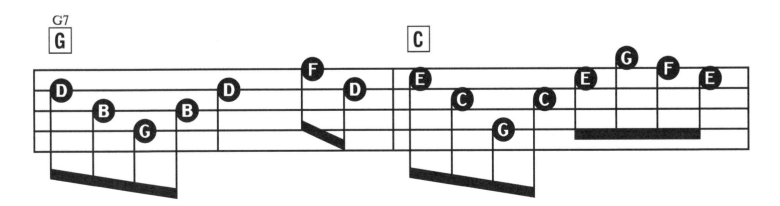

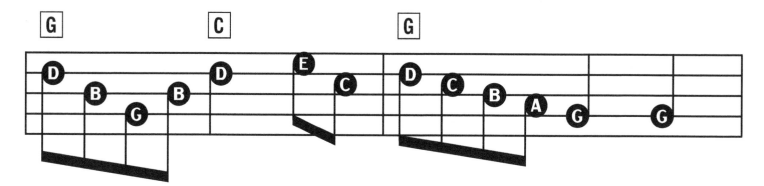

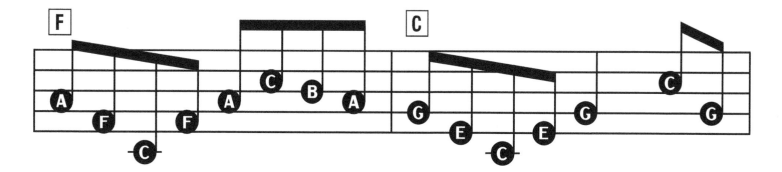

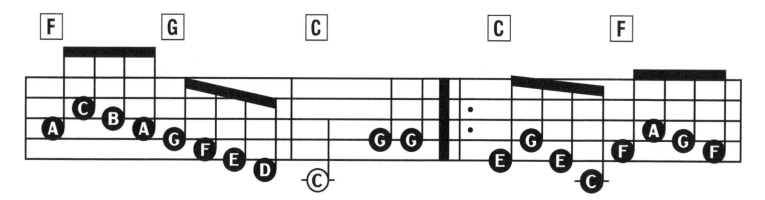

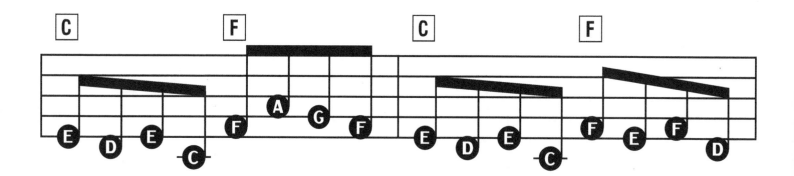

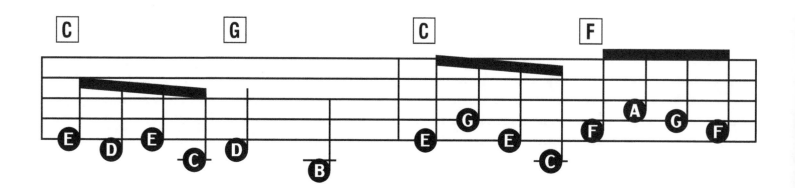

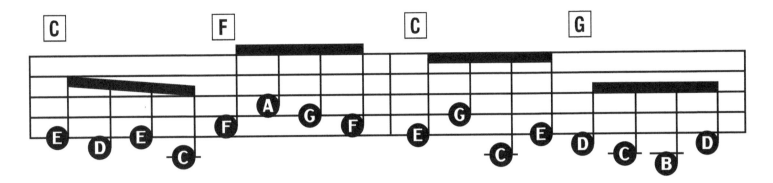

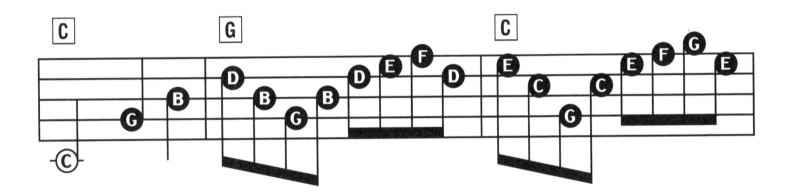

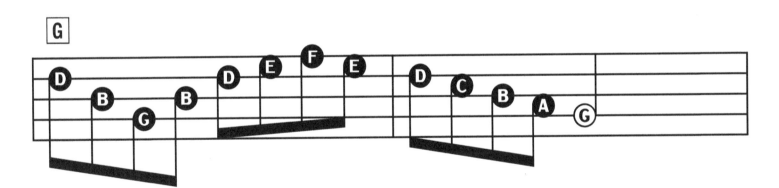

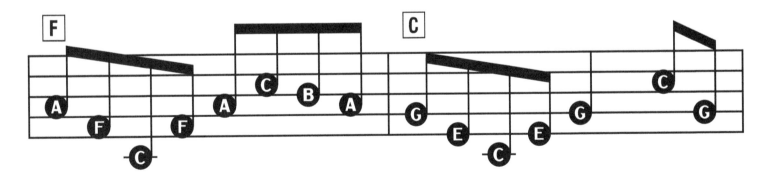

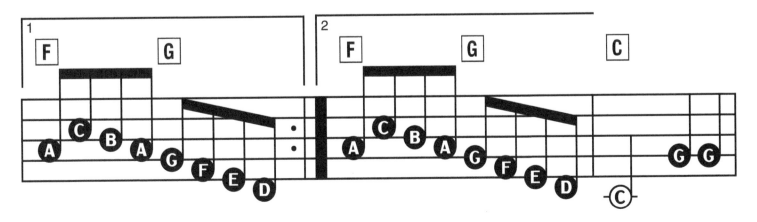

40

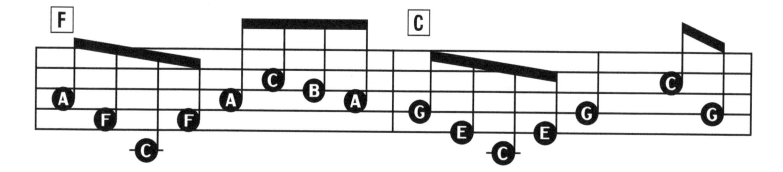

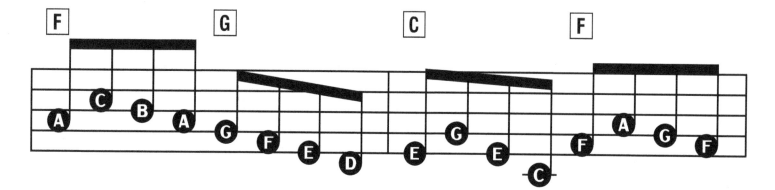

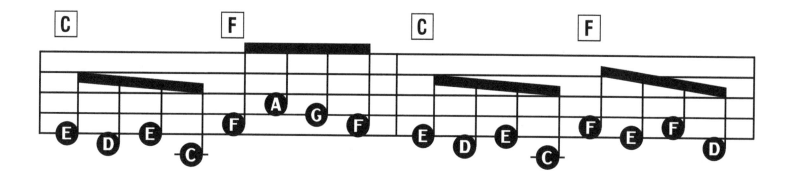

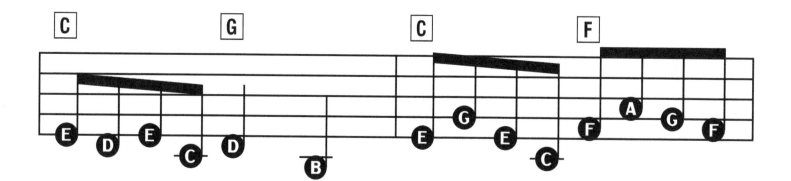

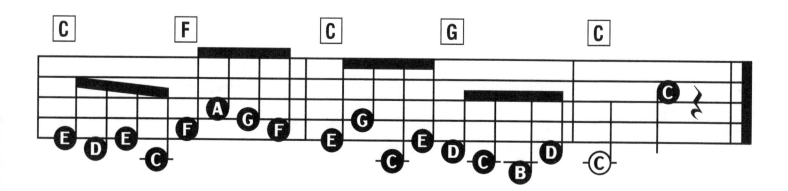